GALACTIC MILK

FREDERICK FARRYL GOODWIN

GALAC-
TIC
MILK

THE FIVE QUESTIONS OF MORTALITY

MIAMI UNIVERSITY PRESS OXFORD, OHIO

MIAMI UNIVERSITY PRESS
356 BACHELOR HALL
MIAMI UNIVERSITY
OXFORD, OHIO 45056

Grateful acknowledgment is made to the following periodicals and books in which many of the poems in this collection first appeared: *The Chicago Review; Buber's Bag Man* (The Gig Press, 2010); UNESCO Anthology: *Le Livre d'or des Poètes de Struga* (*Volume I, Poètes du Monde*, 2011)

Library of Congress Cataloging-in-Publication Data
Goodwin, Frederick Farryl.
[Poems. Selections]
Galactic milk : the Five Questions of Mortality / Frederick Farryl Goodwin.
pages cm
ISBN 978-1-881163-53-4 (acid-free paper)
I. Title.
PS3607.O592265A6 2013
813'.6—dc23
2013032366

FRONT COVER AUTHOR PHOTOMONTAGE:
BRIAN MUSGROVE AND SCRATCH PRODUCTIONS
BACKGROUND: JET PROPULSION LABORATORY
DESIGN AND COMPOSITION BY QUEMADURA
PRINTED ON ACID-FREE, RECYCLED PAPER
IN THE UNITED STATES OF AMERICA

FOR ***LINDA***

&

NATE

CONTENTS

1

2

3

4

5

I come to you as one comes to a phantom, a principle embodied in the flesh.

Still, the neutral angels sing . . .

1

SONG OF SOLOMON

The days belonging to History are unmerciful, Lord
As those still outside it, are unspeakable. Yet once there was a Morning
Missing in Spring, when threads of Flax
Were Woven
to a baby's
shelled skull
&
Lassos of fine spun Light
Were Seen
To
Bind the universal Soul
To this Race
(or that)
While ivory Shell
Was Pulled
From the bed of the sea, and hammered on the Heel
Of soft teething gums

Here, we watched the earth
run
without eyes
into cool wet seas
And
listened
to
the Moon

without ears
catch small-boned fish
with her gay tidal
mouth

We were urchins of light, on our first human Day
sea-spawned creatures of delight
under the ancient Bluffs
which raised their antlers
like a Choir
of clay,
as we rose like rams

under Heaven.

AH, BITTER QUEST

I was sitting by dudley's lake and imaging that this was what
I would have created had there been nothing but me.
first the sights and then the sounds and then the tactile breeze.
some sort of endeavor would capture the one and then there

would follow some other sort of action to catch another
in its net as if butterflies were flying by. some sort of sequence
would follow until the very sense of it could be rolled
up like cinemascope or cigar leaf and smoked. I would

. . .

disappear into each aspect of it so that the woman seeking me
and unable to find the object of her quest would have to go
back to the world I created or allow her heart to be filled
with nothingness or the love she sent out which i returned.

one or another of you might get through from time to time.
rising as in a funnel to an ascending vortex which might accelerate
to a declension of fire. this I would reserve for the
hardcore among you who came up empty.

THE BED

Spring, the green corruption.

To the lips of thy mind will I come like a lover.

And there, annoint the coronation of your head.

Within your heart I have built for you an ark,

and there must you bear me your two sons: one, the (manor born the minor) barbarian of good

the other, hooded, with the sceptre of saints, to announce

the (lesser, major) moons of evil.

SPRING

Within your forehead,
crowd the crow's
bright vistas,
daylight.

Within the cloudburst
of your breath,
blood leopards
lush meadows
Cardinals
the black flower
of night.

Within the pure lotus
of your strength,
horizon's rolling white
length and the sea blue atoll,
of morning.

LILACS

Pungent, sweating, ripening
in the gorge of the blacksmith's
forge, under heaven's vaulting sea,
fleur-de-lis by the intersecting
spires of summer's desire
and winter's white chastity,
they emerge from snow to show
and tell their purple prose
after daffodils have raised
their yellow skirts like debutantes
at spring's great ball, in the nave
and transept, of the Gothic church
of earth.

SNAIL

wherever the Snail is, that is its home . . .

FRANCESCO ANGELITA OF L'AQUILA, 1607

He is the TROJAN HORSE—
left behind in the ship's

hold of Pleiadian garden
slime, neither insect nor

mammal, whose one small
tress of a ship's Manifest

of flesh, on a Spartan
shelf . . .

(could conquer volumes
of the City of G-d's

ten warring factions of
the Sefirot's Higher Self).

Spartan Prince or plodding
hero at history's Ground Zero,

who Sailed the seven seas
for ten long years to crawl

by the frieze of the Garden's
wall, w/ antennae to nebula.

As pure simple truth —
of the UNDERWORLD'S ROOF.

BIKINI

The oleanders shiver in the breeze

their slender white stamens

like the long legged navels

of bright, Spanish

seaside

girls.

SALMON

Pure protein confection
cured to perfect pink,
proteus-muscled,
red Norwegian
king, *livery*
of the
sea.

THEE ECSTATIC

AMORGOS, GREECE

White-caps over dragon ridge
goats,

herding themselves to sleep
fig trees grazing

under ancient leaves

▪ ▪ ▪

2

MOUSE HOUSE

ASSEMBLAGE/FOUND TEXT ON PAPER

The garden at Eichstätt was its secret. No bones about
the circa 1962 Sputnik chandlier, though, which, at the center top of a pristine white wall, was

the focus of waves of adoring pilgrims. The Titans of the 20th-century became the foundation
of the drum-shaped repository. Though space is at a premium

▪ ▪ ▪

inside Mouse House, every centimeter has been put to good use. The barley-twist lamps
and brass lantern are from a Paris flea market. Walking up the farmer's stairs, an indoor

blue tin roof is interrupted by silvery stars and antique sailor's clouds.
When it seemed as if all joy had begun to leave its rooms.

DEPRESSION HOUSE

Centaurs, like crushed velvet birds, call out through the air,
eating berries & roots. I-Penitents in golden groves
blow inland from the sea&sing past the island's

solitary well, where?past the fig trees & hidden
places &therewhere orange ripensin a copse of wild
flowers: hear us sing again to the sound of church bells

▪ ▪ ▪

to toll in the garden trill like the tone of a riverrushlike wind
through pine needles. &In the still night bya pond
w/ lillies,musicalsmoke of dusk, likemusicpollen

rising from a remote kimono. Under mountain mist I spent
my lifeA drowning man on shore, whereI watched
my youth walk slowly past on water.

BUBER'S BAG MAN

Dreams he's pissing into a bottle=on the nimbus that is Jerusalem=by The Damascus Gate:
His mother dancing out front on the grass where she had pep in her steppe

right up until the end when the Gods oh Origami, demons she told im, cut her paper
legs off ah the knees. He waz formed from a single sheet of wet paper, folded

inward where we weeps, the weight of water lapping at the shore line of our matter.
(she told him, wispering)   While I nattered to the whip o wills, a tattered doorman w/ a

tattooed m   heart, spilled vials of poison over the linoleum I laid down over skin, over
the freight o f the page, burned & was blown away. He smoked a pipe full of soap

bubbles, made of His own matter, a crematorium under the moon of each nail. Bullfrogs
croaked from inside the synagogue .[as my seasonal human nature]. Drifterd by.

▪ ▪ ▪ ▪

IF THERE IS A G-D

There cn be little doubt the dead bow down to Him.
And that there is little talk of His exile & alienation. Only a few whispers perhaps

in alleyways of binary logic. The mystery of his calculus & algorithms. Who shall live
& who shall die left to lesser beings. The tsunamis & earthquakes engendering them

▪ ▪ ▪

following in the wake of the Archangels peeling onions by the Dark Tower
of hsi bells. When the synaggogue fill w/ the faithful, there si little talk of differneces.

The continental shelfs once again seem empty w/ out r brothers lives lost at sea.
We can only mutter of His exile & alienation. Whether Allah left his mosque to the whispers.

I was caught up in a maze of Oscar Kokochkas.The Ger man s
w/ their potato mashers to the head. I s w o o n e d in small barbaric rooms.

Even my Brothers were there. It felt worse thn anything I couod have imnagined.
I felt like a *cuckoo clock* w/ its cuckoo guts cut out. When the kale came in //:

■ ■ ■

the place seemed green. The filth feathering the windows knock'd at The Doors. The tokensto
the Alhambra [in L.A.] expired a long time ago. I was working then. Still part of the filthy

system I devised for myself. With my volume and plume still trailing behind me,
I was assigned to a case. Stuffed studs. Eight Balls.

METAPHYSICAL THUMBPRINT: CONTRACT KILLER

I have no name. Only my facial stubble identii\fies me. And the child at play within me. With an ice ax he attempts to scale the walls within. His bald head is ageless and wallows in the muddy

trenches at the heart of me. Without him, I would surely perish, flounder at gunpoint in the commotion of each robbery I commit upon the defenseless villagers who inhabit the perimeter.

The tripwires we have set have all proven useless. Explosives have no effect upon them. They are for all intensive purposes dead. Only the child and myself can lay claim to any hold on this life.

My alibi is that I am absent from all activity even when present. My boots are caked with the mold of the future which hangs in an intricate web fusing all time dimensions into one thimbleful

measurable as a thumbprint at the crime scene. I want off this case. It is unsolvable.

KUROSAWA'S STRAY DOG

FOR ANNE DORWARD

Harumi Namiki, I come to you in handcuffs, remembering my first arrest
a mere circus performer, as my daddy before me, a contortionist

Who swam on the bottom of the Grand Banks, during a Great War
300 feet below the Atlantic Ocean, a strongman walking upright

in irons along its magnetic floor. I wore a pretty dress given me
by a gangster in a white linen suit, who carried a stolen Colt

With a six bullet clip, a stray dog who lived inside of me, and panted
in the long drought and the heat. I became a mad dog (like you, Frederick Yusa), who could only think & see in these straightest of lines.

KUROSAWA'S STRAY DOG

Harumi Namiki, I come to you in handcuffs, remembering my first arrest
a mere circus performer, as my daddy before me, a contortionist

MIZOGUCHI'S BAILIFF

Shanno, I come to you having woken once as a human being, and blinded
by the brilliance which lived inside the slaves I kept in darkness.

In a cave where I kept the 11th century there were songbirds
who sang of the women who flew in and out of me when the bailiff let me go

■ ■ ■

for a walk. Most mornings moored by the lighthouse which sent me diving for abalone
which I sold in the market or traded for children who suffered from hunger in the famine

I did not know that the planets were speaking to one another while I slept
That all the marbles I thought were electrons were circling inside my inflatable raft of a head.

TOMATO VINE

Moist as limbic shoals, I seek the knight's glory: armour of my realm's amorous gambit.
The leash of light which binds its warm body to my own in the noonday sun to marry the

glamorous welts of the lands deep brine in their blind souk: lair to the kingdom.
I salute the Egyptian who flounders in the desert of the ocean's lost sands : loose cannon of faith

in the mouth's itinerant kazoo.
.Torniquet, I beseech you to stop me from bleeding . Corn forms in the crucible of my eyesight

,forlorn rustler on the high plains of my sagebrush ,drifting through the canals . Fatima, I give
you my voice for your shrine, Conchita in the madras noon, high colour for your robust cheeks,

balm to my chagrin in the midnight hour of bright light burning its fabulous hole through the
center of my [ ] coveredbyabannana leaf, to the fig tree growing from my loin cloth of brimstone

flange of blue light, gas off the main to the house about to explode, her slender wrist wipes
moisture off her nether lips, gyre to the unspeakable scope of the sky.

■ ■ ■ ■

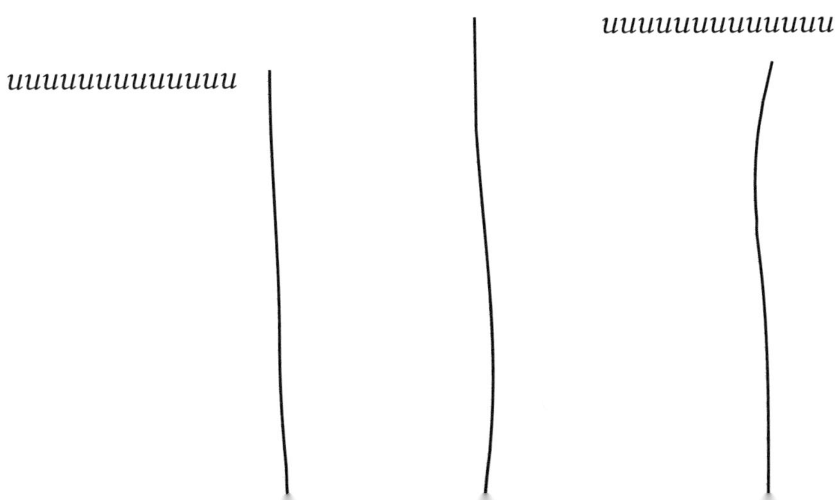

TITMOUSE [IN THE RAIN]

to the rumblings of [my] discontent] : diamonds in the dirt of their sharp sleep.
iiI spit in the eye of the lord to cleanse the oracle within/:. then stutter.kiss myself on both cheeks

distressed flesh in the brokem wing of catastrophich winds. I long for the monsoon and estabkish
a beachhead on cape hattersas. The sun is a torrent of seed today dazzling as she goes blowhole

▪ ▪ ▪ ▪

of the yellow shore. beyond the flotation of the planets [is] the tarpaulin of their distant glory.
shingle the seagulls which shroud the void, shrine in the sleep

of kerosene modernity Λ at the heart of it all:. Two tons of salami on the short stilts
of her fumigation thighs. A city of a woman by the sea shore.

Tit

Tit

Mouse

Mouse

hairlip,

smoke signal at the rainbow;s tattered end. , largesse of a fabulous inheritance fabled mansion
of the sultan's wealth. Old world. at the crossroads ,, combine to the maker's plantings,
[variegated vein through which] the hammer blows of his boiling will flows.
I kkwas deeded this life.vowel rug. homily of maps and pinnacles, arctic expeditions to a
woman's polar regions, the tropical descents boils, its interminable rabid seasons.

3

FOR KAJI ASO

THREE SENRYU

Where the moon sits
on its pale blue branch,
in its bough of morning sky . . .

Where swans float gently by,
the green latitudes of the seasons
shift, fanning their tail of stars . . .

And a child's breath,
blows purple thunderclouds,
over a mountain ridge . . .

FROM ***NOMAD: EZEKIAL'S DIARY***

8111987

I walked back slowly by the elopement of the sea and its brazen adultery
covering the cold arms of heaven. The steeple chased its huge shadow
across the deafening quick of the city's lost cry. Choirs beat
their intemperate rhythms against the fodder of my ribs. Ivory
emblazoned breathed upon the ashen book of earth. To the sea,
my heart leapt and sped with all its might. The iron curtain
of the shore raised its heavy voice and I crawled into the shell of blue
which like an egg surrounded me. Dusk pebbled the crisp sheet of light
smoldering amidst pages belching smoke. In the charnel house of years,
five fathoms deep, a ton of light raced by history's tumultuous shore.
Symphonic in its drizzle of lightning and blood-backed drizzle,
where the delta of the mind once dwelt: here: the great heron's gilded
flight careens carpeting inner night, spirits the body to the great aorta's
granite phantom. Now? Ten gods of the hours of the night hover
by the cypress grove, alternately cursing and spitting. Each by an urn,
in turn, waits. Genuflects ingenuously. Ingloriously.

Blesses me.

4111987

The attraction of pain become visible; the attraction of pain cloaked and
bathed in innocence. Some slow upheaval ties off the cord of life.
Earlier, the hands that swaddled this birth forsook their hold. Lips
which touched, and were mine, pressed upon the gate no longer.
And when I knelt, there was no earth upon which to pray.
Faith and the furnace which stokes two hearts and the fallen souls
who rest within each other's broken solace like brother and sister.
Pain alone cannot vanquish me for I left the throne of
body and senses and touched the forehead of the crown whose
love alone can hide and bear me.

6111987

Birth and the hot spur of flesh anchored to the firmaments rains of hell. Magma and the rot of breath exhaling its rags and oiled lineaments upon the deep swallow of descending stars, penetrant of the magma's untouched heart: in the fire, bless us, constrain our hearts, for we would desert each other in sympathy to your name, for the glory of the word. Behold us in our glory, we speak in eternity, the stars bow down in sadness and sleep.

DRAGONFLY

Biplane ladder in the sky, he is crawling with the other insects through the doom
Of our backyard, demotic socioeconomic demons surrounding him, phantasmal head rotating to inquire of our species why? I am crawling with the other insects through the hives of summer air, with wings veined more delicately than a leaf suspended on a vine of air, I am paused momentarily on top of the bird feeder to observe you as you refill the more feral among us, the birds with whom I share this intricately divided town. Though they are larger, they fly from you unlike my brethren and me who are fascinated with you, the way you move in the world, and pretend at dusk that you a mosquito shaman wearing khaki, moving towards the dark of your demise, at the close of each long day in the hazy doldrums of the hea[r]t you curse, but we are not bats nor beasts nor, as I've already said, your avian neighbors, but mere insects with a mind and an appetite for friendship with your kind when you are able with the butterflies, to be kind and dip yourselves like wax which melts with the waves which blow in from the bottom of the volcano at the heart of all heavens. This we share with you, cater to your confort, observe your amusement, your cruelty in disguise, identify the worst among you who will be brought low at Judgement Day, and be given a pair of wings, surprised to be flying beside us, following on the kidnapped, chalices of drops of jitterbugging red blood.

Mere insect, I crawl through a recollection of atomic ash, a fishmarket contaminated by GI's in the Bikiini Atoll, know doom daily surrounded by death, neighbors with whom we have no quarral but share the riches of dirt, some are indoor dwellers and some languish capaciously out of doors in the heat, when winter comes and drops her scalding white anvils from terrible heights, we fold our biplanes like butterflies and die, crawling from the hives of spring to eat mosquitos who invade your house leeke ronin without a master, asking to commit hara kiri in the courtyard of your dobyin as they did for the first time in the sixteenth century, having pawned their swords in the throes of their poverty, disembowling themselves with bamboo, as each of you will do too on your last day in the summer heat, before your descent into the unclean lips of Isiah, in the cooling jets of fall.

First my hair fell out, then my bones were crushed & rotted, and I asked on a train with other men: "What happened to the Earth?" It's not that it was burning under the weight of demons who walked upon its surface acting as if they were men. No, it's that the sum of a thousand suns were burning inside each of them trying to get out. I tilted my head on its axis to get a better look but it was impossible, for I could not penetrate beyond the surface of the living fires which surrounded me on all sides in the spring. Each year, the molten ones burst into what you call bloom as the love of heaven opened up like a hand upon the breast of her children. The bears and the bees had wanted to go to Brazil to escape the H-bomb along with the ancient owners of the foundry. Then, once it was thought that 400 tons of uranium would sufficiently enrich the thought of mankind that he could escape from his inexorable descent into the slough of the troughs of his own making. But the trees shimmered in response and the green at the center of their hearts committed hara kiri in repose. It was no good in the end. Winter let out its arctic bark l[i]eek an artist gone berserk in a psychiatric ward. Fall stripped the lava lamps from their baroque holders in the walls of summer. What was left was an eternal Spring which fed the hills of Eden and set out with cracked maps for the same shore where the ocean had been rolled up and returned to its original yellow scroll.
I took my place in the zoo of you as I was blotted from the imperial sky.
It was my own decision to proceed down the derelict aisle with the other narcotic narcoleps.

Dope-Hope slatterns riddled the socio-economic grid of modern civiizlaztion with their suspendrs and bow ties. The five principlals of St. Augustine's City of G-d included a kidnapper and pederast, shank bones on the pesach plate of Modern Tomes. This is not the transcription of a dream from the saint of another genretruused up on stilts to rubberize the page, [to inflate the diaphragm of the sage frozen in the page] frozen boomerang bone, papyrus skiff of bamboo swords come to trouble the deep peace of your ritual disemboweling on a public stage where rage came to matter in the sugar fields,

Woman with dildo, 1532

DDDDDDDDDDDDDDDDDDDDDDDDDDDDDDDDD

Woman with dildo, 2032

How far away does the writing happen from here – a million miles from here. And then only when it rains in between the known seasons and blossoms into a void from which I emerge and to which I shall go. But an actor wishes to go with grace from the spoace which he populated. I ewas here for a very long time, it seemed, hoem away from home meant something different to me than to you, I was swept up by a heaven bull to a heavenly height one day to drop my H-bomb of identityon the formless One. I was spat out of paradise in a second and it hurt. For a long time, I was covered on the inside with the barnacles of his Passion. It troubled me as I trembled. It was his love which hurt and bared its teeth which were as breathless as the wind. I swooned, then fell in love. I soldered the iron span between two halves of me to a higher hitch. Posting in the saddle of all four horsemen, I stroked the serpent taking shapeinsdide me, waiting to tqke off its clothes.

I live in fear inside a box within a small room. All my friends whom I melt down to dross at the orifginal foundry are there. Lover Boy, the Pimp with Handlebars, The Leggy One with the Bullion Breasts, Kate from the Village with the twisted bouganavilla. I was swallowing my organs as they rotted out in the heat and spent my time at the Oriental Buizzares trying to sole my feet. I wore high heels to bed when I was young so I could step over the dead who surrounded me on all five sides. I took offence at everything and no one escape d my notice. I had a question, Mark, Jesus was saying to me in a dream. I was living in a hell on earth and wanted to find a path to enlightenment. The Australian skull surgeon ooferred her breasts to my eager mjouth but eschewed the higher demons of my mind who I regarded as lesser saints in the town which occupied the five quadrabts of my heart. I was injured early and life but escaped the fate intended for me. Once I was on my hands and knees pleading for forgiveness. The only one in the crack house who gave an ambulatory damn, was the face peeling off my own from down under.

THE SAFETY PINZER
& UNCERTAINTY DRILLS

FOR TOMMY McGOWAN

Waving in search of the sea and its geographies of interpenetrabilities
(p. 213, Nate's Raworth/Keith Tuma essay), fabulist of myriad tapestries of
Modern Rome's Tacitus,
words even now begin to fall apart, their centers cannot hold, head
scientist of textiles
at the Indian's Wyandotte Worcested Mill, tapping the giggle juice with a
pony of sherry
in New Mexico and purple micro dot, with Oppenheimer reciting
the Vedas as Plank space begins to unfold, boring out his brains with
chopsticks in an oriental crackpit, quoting the Tibbetan Book of the
Dead and the Tao te Ching, lucent lights light the pinkness of her skin,
all extensions of the bed removed her air pressure was increased ten fold
from church and the tremulant of the organ digged into the Rig Vedas,
hypnotized by the theatre and bottom of the manifested universe. Rin Tin
Tin had a can of Red Heart dog food, Professor McGregor at MIT went
to bed, chicken head eaters in Louisaia danced with a feast of snakes,
Kermit LeFleur blended merino into cascading shadow patterns at the
sulpherous satanic mill, whiles Westbrook Pegler broke the heavenly chord
into melodies with his right hand, and with his left played counterpoint by
sawing off his own leg.

LETTERS TO MAGDALENA

I adore you as one adores the whore of abstention. I drove myself mad . with desire for myself. Slept in the cut carcass of a cow, bred bees in the Georgics with Virgil. Fatal.
Feted. Fealty. All collapsed with the vessel I was pouring my self into. As the bottom dropped out. Falling down an elevator shaft. An Otis elevator operator I performed a function. Slipped the sixth heart knot knowingly with the dead. I awke divi[ ]ed in two. Broken into pieces. Whole. Beyond duality. Light lit your face from behind and found me. Talking to a man in the wall. Of mattr. Nobel. Bombared with shrapnel. Fathom down. Your ghair flew with air. Salt in the wound of m.

I came to you in the olive garden from the basalt columns of hell, fresh as a daisy my lyrical hymen intact, noserings flapping in the wind, fire in the hole of my master. Nailed to a cross at sunset I ate myself digested the mongoose that crawled inside the cobra of my senses sawed off the shotgum of my eyes, thickened my to[n]gue with cornstarch, ate my asshole for q halo. M mouthed off to the clergy who threw vbaloons at the sun with an ostich in my crotch which e croched hymens [and ghyms to the cleft palate of my [ineffable brain] . stem[med] from the lurch .

I wanted to loosen my skin to see what oewuld come in.

From their rectums I realized the proverbial horizon of desire was filth when I stepped outside the reptile's palace of the

natural world it was merely pneumatic as an Arab mechanic
then the heart knot dropped into the seventh fold flowering
the final spinal merely killing me and the spirit who occupied
the floored. Smells rose from the sifter of the fields and the world
hung like a sommelier's gold cup around his mile long neck succubus
drinking the blood of the living through [a] painted straw.

Happy happy tulips tulips
Happy tulips Happy tulips happy
happy tulips happy tulips tulips
tulips happy tulips happy tulips
happy
happy
tulips
tulips
tulips happy happy tulips
happy
happy tulips tulips
tu
lips.

Through the [Tonton] macoutes and Duvalier (The Agronomist by Demme)
The shamus cyclone at the center of me spilling outward like a pint of
bitter flowers floored to the ceiling and then the basment tapes and tapas
which did me in outside
The bottom line of me was a hero of a thousand zeroes with baba
bazcinchka calling from my knees with her squids luxuriating in the
profusion of their own mansions of black oily ink

I was drilling holes in the walls of my homunculus in to let the eels in. First
came the Jappanese archetype holding a sword, then the Frenchman who
(stole)ate cupcakes made of milled[from the Japanese girl band calling
Linda Linda linda to three derriers]
Steel, before I new it I was sitting with daneil in a den to let the lions in.
first the fir took
Root in me, and then the sea. With its rinses an d roasts. I was tumbling
down an Icelandic volcano made of ripened rock. Shit-hot I made it to my
knees with a bucket
Of life;s bullets inside of me. I squeeled like a pig til they all ran awy. Then
the mistress
Wreathed in a mustard gas of mint, mists thriygh the door thighs me.i
beat the valuable
Rugs with an old fashioned rug beater. Reptile. Amammal. There was too
much interference to tame all the bees. Zeroes with cunning of zoro cut
me to bits. Razor blades
Sliced my penis in two. One for me. And one for you. I prone to be de-
assholed and leave
My torch in the air. Swimming to the reptile and santa claus inside of
me. Israel was in the air. In my hair. Mouthing the Palestinian inside of
me. who wanted to get out. The Israeli who wanted to escape the fear.
Burnished noosw. Haiian necktie. Maya dervers
Bleeding inside of you. jean Dominique bleeding inside of you. then the
trucks arrived
With poured concrete to plug up the gaps in the rods and cones in the
walls. A bazooka
Firted back from the attic. America holding a garttling gun with an
amazement [amusement]of books,
Boots singing with the Turkish soprano drinking virtual tee with the
Queen.of crooks.

I was running into a problem in the with the Heat. The awful energy of the
counterweights in the form of like the sky.There was “a primitive in a blue

serge suit" [said by a critic of Imamura/the eel], a bizarre litrary gorilla [the bosoton globe ideas section long piece about literary scholars Sunday 5/13/08].ineeded to eat in the tinfush diner which soshi kamikaze ran in his spare time after work. I flew the ccop of the once-overs the voiceovers inside of me I cooked for spare parts. Then the tumor grew big as a yew so my mother and brothers used it to for stew.i mikd the barley at midnight to hear the cricket s calling to the crum bums in cadillacs. At 2 in the morning I ate flapjacks & played craps between wall w/ in the wallpaper flypapered over my knuckles. Bolts of unusable cloth beating wet song with bird song. Then the dawning of [what see m ,ed& I hoped were]the final days.

4

THROAT

I hide behind
a white PICKET

FENCE, gnashing
at my leash,

my coral reef,
of teeth,

in ambush
for the hand's

ripe larder,
the tongue's

fat fodder,
the star

you will
smuggle

over the
border

in a tin
cup for

me,
stored

in a jug
of MILK

and
WATER.

THE ESTATE

An inheritance was left
Consisting of a solid heart

The chambers which pumped
Blood were gone, healed over

The liquid inside it was supposed
To be the milk of human kindness

But spoiled in the open air
Of sharing. Jackals at night

Tore at the flesh of a felled
Beast, tearing meat

From a carcass, a name since
Forgotten, with a scarf

Around its regal neck, as if
It had once dropped a rope

Down a well from above,
Hoping to pull a few

Of us to a higher height.
When the rope broke,

The apparition of wealth,
With ghost, disappeared.

"Bell casters must dig the casting pit"
he declares to his daughters.

▪

Our original falling man w/ a bipolar heart
from his kingdom's twin Towers blazing behind his Castle Walls: Falling apart.

▪

"O Lord, O Queens of Heave n w/ magnetic repulsion "We bless this & consecrate
this bell with holy water, [he tells an audience of wise fools

▪

I, severrere of the butchered traintarck . . . behidn mdy castele walls. I shall wander
in search of love and its gytpsy wounds, the

▪

Legendary female gambler Cordelia . . . witha bugle horn froma rival gang . . .
Gathering spice from the ground beneath her gallows.

▪

You of the butchered
Traintrack, hoboesst in pursiuit of a vane,

▪

"Waht a feast day for the eople", he says, "you'll cast bells".
Pointing to his audience all poor readers with good eyetsight

▪

"I'll paint icons, stuff my mouth with cold hard cash & sufgar ants
till flat warts appear on my hands with all the world's radio bands". For the

▪

Hummingbirds hovering over honeysuckle flosers, grown in the garden of the
Sweve muythical Pagodas [of the Senses] theres a King's ransom, devolved from

▪

The growing of trees bore imperial brances minted
In the Treasury. That you are out of blood's heavy

▪

Watesrs now in the dew drop reflecting a star, cling to me+aanoin t the cactus
Heaven of my suffereing=Lord, Give me: of my agony, lithographs of you(r), my daughters. wrath

GONERIL

Smells of Ancient Rome. Whole Grain Rolls form on the back of her head to cover
the ears of a sow=the horns of a cow=growing like corn=from the barn=in the back of her head.

{{{{{{{{{{{{{{{{{{{{::::::::::::::::::::::::

The wind inside her rustles like a cave of bats at daybreak coming home.
A thousand green acres burns as she eats a pig's intenstines burping in this interview.

{{{{{{{{{{{{{{{{{{{{::::::::::::::::::::::::

She was raised from the dead. Her whisper (has) aboil
All the usual debauchery is there. the traditional bird masks of ancient Roman baths.

{{{{{{{{{{{{{{{{{{{{::::::::::::::::::::::::

Oeuvres of curried monkey. giant-sized stuffed mice in palm oil. If you
climb high enough, the crumb bums may follow the june bugs and cockroaches / into March .

CORDELIA

FOR LINDA

There is a glowworm which shines from your left eyes when you (she) steps
from the water's (edge). vast fields. (vesuvian) pools. recess b(r)eaches
{{{{{{{{{{{{{{{{{{{{:::::::::::::::::::::::::
smoldering in dense blue harnesses of light. by sense of sea & sickness of sense! & a lake of bees
maggots issue from your nostrils tofeed on larvae meat. rotting
{{{{{{{{{{{{{{{{{{{{:::::::::::::::::::::::::
on your gilded skein of beautiful bones. a scaffolding of jewels : the garland
of your smile waves : like a scythe wreathed w/ magpies (keeping the beet?)
{{{{{{{{{{{{{{{{{{{{:::::::::::::::::::::::::
Yyou pretend for amoment to drift downstream (away from me)
We hunker into the ground for shelter = of your will's approaching heat.

IRAQ

oeuvres of curried monkey
ordures of curried monkey
hors d'oeuvres of curried monkey
savorines of curried monkey
choice morsels of curried monkey
bonne bouches of curried monkeybonne

Olde Catullus w/ his off the cuff riffs & one liners
Gaius Valerius Catullus w/ his off the cuff riffs & one liners

GLOUCESTER

Three sirens, peacock landlubbers in blue chiffon, all poor dancers with carnival pitchforks, entice him [to] by the razor of the river's edge / their ragged reedy

cacophonies soaking jasmine roots to determine if his ancestors had a space for him in their cemetery. in the end so what was the point of stuffing my mouth with

▪ ▪ ▪

sugar ants. Even my eyes haunted me when I put them out with lye. For a while, I survived as a preacher, then tried my hand at emotional extortion along with my

sidekick Sirk. But in the end something callous and calamitous would happen to everyone I knew. But, never having been, I would not be one of them.

Madness hangs in the balance of a well which lords over the realm ofearth. The men of Auvignon hang in the balance of a boy whose Holy Mother is Rome, “monster of carrion” “the cardinal is cannonized” as the head of Austria hangs from a hag’s pole called war. The child is monstrously fruited by the Nature hidden in the budding sacks which fall from Fortune and are our ruin of pestilence. A wife cries out that in her time her faierer fortune that should live shoul be her death and another mother that her rapture’s kindgdom of Jeffery in Arhtur does live befr ethe third eye pluckest by the enormity of enmity which between two halfs of the same heart bear for one another. Civil in civil war is the palimsest of manners which flowers like thehanderchiefs of court remonstonce of this other monstrous striving of the breast of man., That he shoud be a man if actction not of cword and cut a cord of word from his brother’s limbs, That with this he should keep jis warmth, hi husband in her moth, and that hose words hich wrre born in his mouth should fly like a wren to a heavenly nest to ask for pardon for eaxh our blood sins thninng the love with twhich we were stn to meet, lovem, fall before the menses and jungle of the icon of our othering mothers. The waggle dance in the bee hive. The hyp e of our impact as icons fo our world and asphalt tkings. Did he not hop to make each of his sons live and limbs.

5

SEASONS PASSING

SILENCIO Y EL MUERTE AZUL

Silence, and the blue death
Of night, when silver fish
Swim through white depths,
To the tranquil heart of the moon.

It is the last day of my life.
The last day of the light.
The final day sleeping,
In the red wine of the sky.

LABIA MAJORA

Loitering out of water:
Lungfish. Memento mori,
Urn of aquatic ash, bright
Warriors circling:
The oasis of a burial-herd.

In the Angel's Book of Mecca:
A vulcan strides the leaded
Garden, glimmering of jewels,
Cistern of deep waters, the molten
Exhalation of land,

The tribe's delirium hive.

In memmoriam, the smelting
Iron of the giant asleep.
At the centre of the Earth,
The scarlet summit, a supplicant's
Scrolled hibiscus, scimitar's hair-lipped
Shrine, or seraphic
As an unearthly dream
Still odorous as Creation's first day,
Gelding the tribe forward

To an epoch enshrined.

STILL LIFE WITH TECHNICOLOR VULTURE

The head is a TURK'S CAP LILY,
more red than orange, granted,

but spotted with the BLACK-EYED
SUSAN of TWO IRIS. Red flesh wound

nautically in a turban shaped knot.
Sultan of swing. "Goddess Isis."

Gasped asp. CERASTES CORNUTUS
painted on a blue wall.

Of an earthen jug or sarcoph
agus; this wild red rose.

Rotarian or votive candle,
shaved above the black tutu

of its black smock. And DIS
CURSIVE SCRIPT.

WASP

The stylus is scratching a DVD+R of the natural world crumbling in the heat, abdomen connected
sprouting leaves of wings, a cluster of legs folded in two perfect pairings,
the joints delicate as gold

Gloves & the long legged arachnid like feet emerging as if sprouting from the shaft of a weathered
brown leaf, boom vang, brown pod. The head is a triangle of mottled tans
& browns with antennae

Folded & dried like the short legs beneath the neck which fly by in stillness with the
second hands. The eyes are marvelous brown jewels, kind and oversized as if a
fluttering of the wings in all their oversized

Glory could divine the mystery of their design. Squatting on a desk top with another
beggar of alms, we are at treetop for the honey secreting from the haze of blue skies
on a summer day. Drying out w/ age.

WASP II

He was ordering Beluga caviar and Dom Perignon 55 at a seaside restaurant outside a casino saying: please listen to me, it will just take a second: I met him on the island of Capri where he had a brother named Francois, a Franciscan friar, who dined on olives on a beach with wild horses where the Rhone emptied into the ocean, holding onto the white mane of a horse below the waves of the raging sea. He sailed with his long lost brother, the love of her androgynous life, and once came up for air in the cold of winter to say that she'd rather dance. I answered /so would I.

WASP III

He was wearing the butt end of bee balm in his buttonhole, sea anemone from the
ocean floor, honeycomb pattern with a coupling of winged stingers not unlike his own,
the flies descending on his legs for the nectar of sweat. The red flower with its secretions tunneling
into the hive of kings above burnt ember, a shisper of a whisper with its
summer ships protruding with the lark, red as 40's lipstick but with an undercurrant as
sweet as anything he'd previously entered, the remenants of a '64 Padron Anniversario
curling into the ether of the Principe of Monaco, a few girls he'd met on a train trailing
off into memories of tail froma long prehistoric time eons [egosago.

SEFERIS

of the poet . . . it is the cypress tree
that will sprout on his grave
NIKOS ENGONOPOULOS

Finally, the dark cut
flowers are gathered

in their serpentine
vase, while night

holds its meridien
of mules like fuel

on steep stone
steps leading from

the common harbour,
panniers heavy with

(his soft black) stars
tilting at the cosmos

to wonder: who was
it that once hovered

by the hour's mystery
to wander the pitch

(and roll) of olive
groves, as we mourned

by his painted bowers,
the soul of the Cypress sea.

PEACOCK

In essence, the poet has one theme:
his live body.
GEORGE SEFERIS

Eighty pounds of head torqued-tight,
blind as a god,
Shovelful of face, he shovels—
to the sanctity of flesh.
Swilling his blood-pint
Threading his way forward,
along the outback machete-
mouthed along the glacial
tightrope of the spine
Scowling, skull-scarred
the mutant head *pinched* open:
An SS Guard
crouching
under a fur helmet

Like a hirsute hurricane.

Et tu Deum: He Kingdom Comes
swiveling on the quarterpounder-
balls of his divinity,
The steel wrecking-ball head
chauffeuring the body

behind him, like a two-legged-nurse
in-a-hearse, and the fat bullet-
neck straining to slam twelve men
strong (minyon-muscled)
into the incandescent
chapel, of the cunt's
bored rim.

Caecus aque queum Deus:
A black-bellied
Wasp
sporting,
a twelve inch prehistoric sting
of Mesozoic wing. Nerve-caged, entering
long-legged the chink between worlds,
spiraling head-wards, the dark fruit,
primeval gourd, a COLOSSUS
MINUET, and the train
robber stocking, wallpaper-of skin*
Doped as huge as history,
a Voltage acrobat.
You can find him under REPTILE,
in the file for erectile,
in the KING JAMES' BIBLE.
By a slag heap of diction,
sired by friction, riding bareback
in a stable of unconsummated flame.

He is loved fired back to the half-truth of fiction
A pit boss of pits,
gone to seed :: backhoe drawn delicately
to *luminous* deed

An SS Guard,
w/ a pig iron heart : playing
aeolian harp

A black tong of x-box voodoo ::::

a shovelfulof Her heavenly grace.

GENESIS

For whenever a thing changes and quits its proper limits,
at once this change of state is the death of that which was before.
LUCRETIUS

Death-spoked and harnessed
To the manger of the sea:
I emerged, cribbed to the moon's two tusks
Of ivory.
I am dazzled white!

And have worn the sunset's
Red helmet to bed
For an Eternity,
Against the onslaught
Of the stars.

I have yet to burn
The moon back to incense
And silver,
Or swallow whole forests
Beneath the ceiling

Of the sea
Perhaps, if there's time,
I will thresh white
Stone
in my sleep.

#4

SOLITUDE

Moon
drops ash
on empty
skies

fire
fills
the bowl

Moths
ascend
. . .
in
solitude

#4

SOLITUDE

Moon
drops ash
on empty
skies

fire
fills
the bowl

Moths
ascend
. . .
in
solitude

RAPTURE 3

SOLITUDE

Moon
drops ash
on empty
skies

fire
fills
the bowl

Moths
ascend
. . .
in
solitude.

SNOW

FOR DAVID & MARIE-ROSE

It's the gentleness,
with which it flows
downstream.

Millet of cloud,
white vertigo
of seed.

Dust atoms falling,
on a white Sahara
of dream.

UNTITLED [#3]

An arm
reaches out
to write:

It is the tender arm,
of the gardener.

A hand,
a strong hand,
moves across the page. . .

Moving from side to side,
like a pickhoe
moving from row to row.

Tearing gently
into the parched, untried
top-unturned topsoil.

I stoop,
to kiss the page:

the white earth.

The lips,

of the white earth.

This is no time to speak.

To light up posthumously,

leeke a word

The author would like to thank the following:

LINDA *without whose love, friendship, & infinite kindness this book could not have been written*

NATE DORWARD, *my editor, co-author & whose book this is*

JEFF CLARK, DESIGNER WITHOUT PEER

PROFESSOR FERID MUHIC

DR. DAVID SCHENCK

PATRICK LEPETITE

DAN WARBURTON

DAVID, A FRIEND

PROFESSOR SAM & ARLENE BERNSTEIN

PETER BROWN

TOMAŽ ŠALAMUN

KATHLEEN SPIVACK

JOHN LATTA

ROXANNE CARTER

TIMOTHY DONNELLY

THURSTON MOORE

TOM, MADELEINE & JOHN DIMITROFF

RAY DINITTO

STANLEY STERN

BRAM GOODWIN

ANDREA CAGAN

FRED ERLICH

FREDERICK FARRYL GOODWIN

WAS BORN IN 1953 IN FRAMINGHAM, MASSACHUSETTS, AND MATRICULATED AT BROWN UNIVERSITY AT AGE 27. FOLLOWING A STRING OF ODD JOBS, HE BECAME THE VOCALIST FOR THE HARDCORE BAND BLACK HOLE, AND THEN MOVED TO THE U.K., GRADUATING WITH AN M.A. FROM CLARE COLLEGE, CAMBRIDGE. HE IS THE AUTHOR OF VIRGIL'S COW (MIAMI UNIVERSITY PRESS, 2009) AND THE CHAPBOOK BUBER'S BAG MAN (THE GIG PRESS, 2010). HE COLLABORATED ON THE CD COMPENDIUM MALEFICARUM III (INCUNABULUM RECORDS, 2008), A SPOKEN WORD/ELECTRONIC MUSIC COLLABORATION WITH THE COMPOSER DAN WARBURTON. HE WAS INVITED TO REPRESENT THE UNITED STATES AT THE UNESCO SPONSORED STRUGA POETRY EVENINGS IN STRUGA, MACEDONIA IN 2009.